High on
Hope

To Jaclyn ~
May God bless you with
peace and strength
and may you always
have Hope!
So glad I got the
chance to meet you ☺.

Blessings,
Nanci
Hebrews 6:19

High on Hope

Nanci Cosby Johnson

authorHOUSE®

AuthorHouse™
1663 Liberty Drive
Bloomington, IN 47403
www.authorhouse.com
Phone: 1-800-839-8640

The names in this book have been changed to protect the innocent.

Published by AuthorHouse   02/11/2012

ISBN: 978-1-4685-4077-2 (sc)
ISBN: 978-1-4685-4076-5 (hc)
ISBN: 978-1-4685-4075-8 (ebk)

Library of Congress Control Number: 2012900341

To God

The Hope of all Hope

To Mom and Dad

For never giving up Hope

To Robbie and My Girls

For the Hope they provide

To all the sweet family and friends who have loved and encouraged me along life's journey—I thank God for each and every one of you!

Durant, Oklahoma 1996

Her heart was beating fast as she stepped outside the mobile home. Something within her said she shouldn't be there. She was with her boyfriend and her roommate, but fear gripped her heart: She knew she was in an unsafe place. Almost everyone at the party was tripping shrooms, including her roommate. She had gone outside to get away from the party. Two girls who had threatened her before were at the party and, due to the verbal communication spoken loud enough for her to hear, she knew they were planning something. Sure enough, when she stepped outside, they quickly followed. As one of them screamed at her, calling her every name imaginable, the other one slammed her hands into her chest, knocking her to the ground into a puddle of mud. Her boyfriend attempted to stop them, but the fact that she was with him at all only made things worse—he had once dated one of the girls before.

For that reason, the girl hated her for being with him even though they had been broken up for some time. As she started to get up, her roommate started to scream at her too, and for a good twenty minutes, she stood there enduring the insults that were breaking her heart with every word. She was scared and felt so alone. She took off walking barefoot down the gravel road in front of the house. She didn't know where she was going. She didn't even know where she was, but everything inside of her cried out for her mom to come and rescue her. Under her breath she said, "Please Mom, just drive by . . . I know you don't know where I am, but please come and get me." Her boyfriend eventually convinced her to come back to the party, promising her that everything was fine. The rest of the night was without incident, but rejection burned in her heart, and she began to truly understand what it felt like to be the outsider.

I have shared my story many times in various settings, but a twenty-minute testimony doesn't begin to touch the heartache one feels in the midst of a life of desperation. It doesn't touch the hurt that fills every ounce of one's being, and it doesn't even come close to the heartbreak a family goes through when a child has gone astray. I hope this book will capture the hearts of those who have struggled with fear and rejection and be an encouragement to continue their journey to freedom! As someone once said, **"God comforts us, not to make us comfortable, but to make us comforters."** Though my journey has been hard, I am very grateful today, grateful for God's love and forgiveness. My story would be meaningless without His VICTORY! He is my Rock and my Salvation. May I always live the life that brings hope to others!

Chapter 1

As a preacher's kid, you are both blessed and cursed. Blessed with the love, prayers, and support of a church family but also cursed by the stereotype that comes with it. Everyone expects you to do the right thing at all times. A typical Sunday morning for me when I was a child: "Nanci, where do you find that in the Bible?" my Sunday school teachers would ask; "I bet Nanci can name all the disciples," my classmates would say; "We want Nanci to be on our team for Bible Trivia," my friends would plead. They soon learned that just because I was a preacher's kid did not mean I knew the Bible front to back! In fact, I was much more interested in what my girlfriends had in their purses, or what kind of snack we would be having that day, or what my mom was making for lunch. Heck, I probably didn't even have my Bible with me! But that was the typical perception of a preacher's kid, and I'm sure I was a disappointment to some of those sweet little Sunday school teachers.

Although I wasn't your "know-everything-in-the-Bible" preacher's kid, I was still very aware of God's love for me. Growing up I never really lacked for anything. I was the youngest of three and had a very loving family. One of the biggest blessings of being a preacher's kid is the support of your church family. My mom said when I was a baby I would come home from church smelling like a thousand different perfumes from all the ladies who had held me. I have this visual of being passed down the pews, from one lap to another, being prayed over by each and every woman. My mom says, "In a way, Nanci, you were everyone's baby." I was lucky to have so many people who cared about me. I was loved and cherished by both my biological family and my church family, and was very blessed to be raised with a foundation of faith.

I was born in Borger, Texas, and lived in Amarillo for the first five years of my life. My dad pastored Trinity United Methodist Church, and my mom was a stay-at-home mom.

The parsonage was right next door to the church and even had the same pink brick. I don't remember very many details of the house since I was pretty young, but I do remember bits and pieces.

I know our house was really close to a busy street because I remember hearing the traffic outside. I'll never forget one night: Two men on a motorcycle were hit by a car and ended up in our yard at the side of our house. Both were hurt and bleeding, and my dad ran inside to get blankets for them. I don't remember what happened after that—I was only four years old—but what an impact that must have had on me to remember it after all these years. I think what I remember most is my mom and dad's willingness to help someone in need.

That was just a good example of my parents' compassion. Not just my parents but my grandparents as well. My family believed that it was our job as Christians to show Christ's love and always help people in need. They loved God and were devoted to sharing His love with others around them—most importantly their three children.

My parents were always very supportive of me and believed that I would go far in life. I was born with a passion for people. God blessed me with that passion even as a child. I always stood up for the underdog, encouraged those who were in need, and wanted everyone I met to live life to the fullest. I loved life and wanted to grow and be the best that I could be. That was my attitude and that's the way I lived—enjoying every moment.

I think both my brother and sister would agree that we were all blessed to have a childhood filled with wonderful memories. I was very close to both my older brother and sister. My brother, David, is five years older than my sister, Carmen. Carmen is twenty-one months older than I. They were the people I looked up to the most. Even though there was an age difference between us, we still had so much fun together. We used to play soccer in the hallway together and outside on occasion. Dave would play soccer outside for hours. Carmen and I played out there as long as we could, but after a while—it never failed—one of us would say, "I need a drink of water." The other would follow with "Me too," and once inside the house, we had no plans to go back outside. Dave, however, didn't figure out our "escape plan" until much later! He still gives us a hard time about it to this day.

Carmen and I were typical sisters. We loved each other so much, but we fought quite a bit too. We were also pretty good at getting in trouble together. One day Carmen and I, along with our friend Jacy from down the street, decided we were going to spray paint our play house in the back yard. Carmen had left-over spray paint from her science fair project, and we had it all planned out. We had asked our mom if we could paint the house, and her response was, "No, wait until your dad comes home and ask him." We were disappointed because we had been excited about our project. Afraid dad would tell us "No," we went with the theory, "Forgiveness is easier than permission!" So we went ahead with our plan and painted the play house. When mom found out she told us that dad was on his way and that we would have to tell him what we had done when he got home. Carmen and I were scared to tell him, but we had no other choice. We waited in our room until he got home; he came and sat on the bed and we made our confession. Expecting him to be furious with us, we were pleasantly surprised when he took us both in his arms and forgave us. His words to us: "Jesus forgives us of our sins so we should forgive others." Funny, of all the times I got in trouble growing up, that's the one I remember most, and what a great lesson of love and grace that was for us.

After moving to Tulsa in 1985 and living there for two and a half years, we moved to Mustang, a town close to Oklahoma City. My dad had been appointed senior pastor at Mustang United Methodist Church. We moved in the spring of my first grade year. I was excited about moving to the city. Having never been to Oklahoma City, I pictured it like the New York City postcards with all the tall buildings. People who live in New York would probably crack up if they knew I compared Oklahoma City to New York City! The things you learn as you get older.

My new school, Lakehoma Elementary, offered a world of new possibilities. Wonderful teachers, who encouraged my involvement in class activities and projects, bolstered my esteem and love for the arts. Making new friends was never a problem for me as I was excited about being the new kid in first grade and had no fear of rejection. It was a time when I could be myself, outgoing and cheerful, eager to learn and live life to its fullest. Driven by perfectionism, desiring to do my best, I could have easily become an overachiever.

I also made friends with a girl at church named Christy. We had lots of fun. We played on the same soccer team and spent almost every weekend together. We were both bossy and thought we ruled her neighborhood. One time we were down the street at a friend's house and decided to play with the Ouija Board. We had forgotten the fact that we were going to have to walk back to her house in the dark! So when the time came, we held hands and screamed all the way home. She was my buddy. That's probably where my love of jigsaw puzzles came from—we would stay up all night doing puzzles on her kitchen floor. We cried when we found out she would be transferring to another elementary school. We stayed in touch, but I missed not having her there.

Fifth grade was probably my most memorable year. The last year of elementary school we had earned the privilege to participate in all the fun activities, such as safety patrol, hosting the school carnival and weekly D.A.R.E. visits from Officer James Ward. I was even selected by the art teacher to paint a ceiling tile for the cafeteria, an honor given to only two students from the fifth grade, a boy and a girl. I was the lucky girl that year! I painted a baldheaded clown with a hat. Why I chose that I have no idea. To this day it hangs in the cafeteria.

Even though I really enjoyed art and music, my favorite activity was the weekly visits from the D.A.R.E. officer. D.A.R.E. stands for Drug Abuse Resistance Education, a program offered to elementary students to warn them about the dangers of drugs. One of our class assignments was to write an essay for a D.A.R.E. project stating why we would never do drugs. The student with the best paper would read it at the D.A.R.E assembly later that year. I worked hard on that paper and hoped like everything that mine would be the one chosen. After a class vote, my best friend and I tied for first place. To break the tie, the class voted again. I voted for Melissa, assuming she would vote for me as well. Unfortunately, I was wrong . . . she won the competition by one vote . . . my vote!

Just one of those lessons in life—sometimes you need to vote for yourself.

That D.A.R.E program was very important to me. I looked up to our D.A.R.E. officer and hung on his every word. Officer James Ward was the authority on everything, and I often told my parents, "Officer James Ward said this," "Officer James Ward said that." I'm sure they got tired of hearing how "wonderful" Officer James Ward was, but to me, he was a hero. Then one day, my dad and I were driving to the Western Days Parade and I saw Officer James Ward getting ready for the parade. Immediately I said, "Dad, Dad look! It's Officer James Ward. He's my D.A.R.E. officer, Dad look . . ." Just then I noticed he was smoking, and it absolutely crushed me. All the excitement had left my voice and I said, "Dad . . . he's smoking . . ."

I couldn't help but be disappointed that day. One of my heroes, a man I really looked up to, was not the person he said he was. That would be one of my first hard lessons in life: Things are not always what they seem. Thankfully, I had been taught that, even though things change, God's love is sure and unfailing, not just for the person who's disappointed but also for the person who caused it. That was the message my parents and family taught me from day one—a message of hope and endurance. Two things I would desperately need as my journey continued.

Chapter 2

When middle school came around I was excited to be out of elementary school and on my way to the teenage years. I was eager to meet new friends and see all of my friends from elementary school and couldn't wait to see what middle school was like. We were going to have so much fun!

I met my best friend Nicole when I started at Mustang Middle School. I was assigned to a locker right next to hers, and we quickly became best friends. In fact, we were inseparable. If I wasn't at her house spending the night with her, she was at my house spending the night with me. We had so much fun together watching movies, doing makeovers, making home videos, and playing Barbies (even though we would never admit that to our friends at school!). We participated in many of the same activities like pep-club and mat-maids for the wrestling team. We also went to the same church. I often went to the lake with her family during the summer, and we would have a blast. (Feeding minnows to the fish they had already caught would often get us in trouble from her dad and his friends, but we felt sorry for them!) Nicole was very special to me, and I was very thankful for her friendship during my middle school years.

I had my fair share of pre-teen drama—broken hearts, arguments with friends, peer pressure, and all the other fun stuff that comes with being an adolescent. But for the most part, those were fun and innocent years I will forever treasure in my heart. In fact, one of my fondest memories was when I went on a summer mission trip with my youth group. We were on our way back home from Wichita, Kansas, and stopped at another Methodist Church to spend the night. Our youth group got settled in, grabbed our Bibles, and sat on our sleeping bags together as our youth pastor shared his message with us. I will never forget the Bible scripture he shared that night. "Therefore, if anyone is in Christ, he is a new creation; the old has gone, the new has come!" (II Corinthians 5:17).

Immediately, I fell in love with that scripture. It spoke to me in a way that no other scripture had. It was like a revelation for me. It was more than a scripture memorized at Vacation Bible School, it was the Word of God falling on my ears, as if to say "Nance, this is your scripture." I had no idea at that time what my future held, but looking back now, it's very clear that God was preparing me. In fact, when I was in college years later, I had to do a report on my life starting with my birth. When I was doing research, I found the baby announcement my parents sent out when I was born. Right above the hand-drawn baby carriage, drawn by my dad, were these words ". . . behold the new has come." It was the same scripture I fell in love with on that youth trip. It was incredible to me that God had given me that scripture as a baby and has continued to bless me with it throughout my life. Several years ago, I was able to do an oil painting to capture and express my testimony using that scripture.

God also blessed me with a great youth pastor, Brian Minietta. I was very close to him and looked up to him as a role model. I loved going to church and being a part of the youth group. I didn't consider all of them really "good" friends, but we were all pretty close. We had a connection, something in common that allowed us to relate even though we were in different places in life. God was our common factor, and that's what brought us together. They were my youth family.

It was about this same time in middle school I realized not everyone had a strong support system like I had. And not everyone had the desire to follow God. Some of the kids I hung out with at school would tell me about everything that was going on in their home life. I was shocked. I couldn't imagine not having a peaceful home full of love and didn't realize how lucky I was. I was probably just a little naïve and innocent during those years, but my heart hurt for those people, and I wanted to help them.

When I was in the eighth grade, my family had its own reality check. My fifteen-year-old sister found out she was pregnant. Our family had never really gone through anything like that. I didn't know what to expect; I just knew it was a bittersweet time. Although we were excited about little Kindall who was to be born the next spring, we were also heartbroken for my sister. We knew her carefree teen years would soon be replaced with the responsibility of being a teen mom.

It was hard on everyone. I'll never forget the night my sister told my parents. After hugs, tears, prayers, and reassurance that God would see us through, all five of us—my parents, my brother, my sister, and I slept in the same bed together and fell asleep with tears in our eyes. What a bonding moment for our family. We were determined to stick together and support my sister in every way, even though we knew it would be hard.

My parents felt they should be the ones to tell our church family about Carmen's pregnancy and to do it as soon as possible. Unfortunately, my dad had to be out of town that next Sunday. It was hard on my mom to stand in front of the church and share the news with the congregation, but the church unanimously offered love, prayer, and support.

A lot of things changed that year for Carmen and for all of us. Right before school started, my mom took us school-clothes shopping. Usually that was a fun experience for us girls, but this year was different. Instead of Carmen being able to buy the trendy outfits that everyone was wearing, she had to buy maternity clothes. Carmen was angry, my mom was upset, and I felt bad for being able to buy normal clothes.

Now you have to understand, by this time in our lives, Carmen and I didn't exactly agree on everything, and there wasn't much that we didn't fight about. But she was my big sister, and when she hurt, I hurt. Of course, we were all excited about having a brand-new baby in the family; who wouldn't be? But it was still hard for us to watch my big sister give up her childhood and prepare to become an adult at the young age of fifteen.

One day, Carmen and I went to visit my dad in the hospital where he was having surgery on his ankle. We decided to go to the nursery wing of the hospital to see all the little babies. We stood there at the nursery window, looking at the tiny hands and feet of all the sweet babies who had just been born. How exciting, I thought, we're going to have one of those! Carmen is going to be a mom, and I'm going to be an aunt. My head was flooded with all the fun and joy we would have. Looking back, I don't remember Carmen saying much as we stood there. I wonder now what she was thinking that day. Something that was supposed to be a joyous celebration of life was probably so scary for her as a teenager. I'm sure she longed to have a happy home and family, but she knew the reality of her situation. Though she did her best to stay positive, she knew it was going to be a difficult journey.

That year was full of transition. Carmen had her baby, I was anticipating high school, and my brother was in his third year of college. Though we all went our different directions, we were still just as close as a family. We cherished the times that we spent together. My new baby niece, Kindall, brought so much joy to our lives with her sweet little spirit and cute chubby cheeks. She was adorable.

My sister was a good mom from the start and did a great job taking care of Kindall. We would take turns helping Carmen and spoiled Kindall every chance we got. There was a lot of joy within our home with Kindall being there, but there was a lot of tension too. Carmen was having issues with Kindall's dad, and my parents were trying to help in every way they could. It's hard enough to raise and protect a daughter, but it's even harder when there's a grandbaby right in the middle.

So with my parents focused on Carmen and Kindall, and my brother off at college, I wasn't really sure where I fit anymore. Everything was changing, and it was hard for me to find my place. I would be starting high school that next year, so there was another change right around the corner. A change I wasn't sure I was ready for.

Chapter 3

When I started as a freshman in high school, I was bound and determined to do well. I remember being a bit insecure and worried about the typical stuff—not being able to find my classes, making new friends, what clothes to wear, would I fit in? But, nevertheless, it was new and exciting. I would be in school with my sister and her friends and it would be so awesome!

I remember walking from class to class seeing some of the older kids smoking by the cafeteria. Some of my friends were even smoking at that time. It was funny to me because one day someone asked me if I wanted a drag of their cigarette. I was like "No way!" I couldn't believe they thought I smoked! Of course, I didn't smoke. I loved the high school atmosphere way too much to give in to that kind of peer pressure. I was also active in volleyball and knew I needed to focus on school. I wanted to stay eligible to play. I was a leader, not a follower, and I didn't want to be in the "in crowd" if that was part of it.

One night I confronted my sister at a football game when someone told me she was smoking. I was so mad at her; I couldn't believe she was smoking. I was sad and disappointed. First, Officer James Ward and now my sister. I didn't want my big sister to smoke. I remember the girl she was with saying, "Nanci, it's not that big of a deal." And I think my words back to her were, "Well yeah, she's not your big sister either."

I had no intentions of ever smoking; I had no intentions of doing a lot of things. But peer pressure has a way of breaking you down even when you don't see it. So when a girl in one of my classes offered me a cigarette in class one day, I accepted. I put it in my bag and took it home with me. When I got home from school, my parents weren't there, so I went out on the front porch and smoked my first cigarette. Of course, my sister was there and told me I wasn't doing it right—that's a big sister for you! But for me, that was my first step into freedom. Finally, I was going to be like everyone else. How quickly my determination of being a leader and standing apart faded into the feeling of just wanting to belong.

As I write these words, I wish I could go back and start over. One choice at a time, I fell into deception, and it wasn't long before I had lost all motivation. I started smoking in the bathroom with friends, skipping school to get high, and going to parties when I could get past my parents. I even started failing every one of my classes and spending most of my time in detention. It was a new world for me, and though I knew it wasn't a good thing for me, it was a lot easier to NOT care . . . and besides everyone else was doing it. I now despise that cliché because that's the last thing I want to be—like everybody else! But when you're fifteen, one thing you do not want to be is the outsider.

So the story begins. Pinocchio ignores his conscience. The prodigal son chooses greed. And I lose my direction. Was this a sudden change? Absolutely not. Like I said, with every wrong choice I made, I fell further into darkness. Like my dad often said, "It's hard to remember your task of draining the swamp when you're up to your neck in alligators." My alligators were peer pressure, low self-esteem, and the longing to be important. In fact, when I started dating a junior who played on the soccer team, I *did feel* important. Here I was, a freshman dating a junior, and I was falling in love. I still remember the way he smelled, the scent of the winter-fresh gum he chewed, and his Green Bay Packers starter jacket. The way his eyes looked right through me melted my heart. Sure, I had plenty of boyfriends up to this point, but nothing like this! This made me feel extremely excited and really nervous at the same time. We went on a few dates with my sister and her boyfriend and wrote notes back and forth. He would meet me after class when he could and kiss me before he would run off to his next class. One time we passed each other going and coming from soccer practice, and he put his hand on my hair and tousled it back and forth. It was so sweet. I saved every note he wrote me, every candy wrapper or souvenir from our dates. I had a shoebox full of little stuff that made me think of him. I was so excited when he asked me to prom. As a freshman you can only go to the prom if you are asked by a junior, so I was set.

It was around this time that my parents found out my dad would be transferred to a church in Durant, Oklahoma. We would be moving that summer. I was sad in a way, but excited too. I wasn't worried about losing my boyfriend; I was already planning a long distance relationship. I don't think I realized at that time how much my life would change. I just figured I would still be close to all my friends but make new ones too. I was writing all my friends letters to tell them how much I would miss them, even old boyfriends. I liked having something exciting to talk about. I would be moving that summer—so cool! Well, that was before my boyfriend came up to me after class one day and said, "I can't take you to prom because you skipped school."

I knew that wasn't right because it was during study hall, and we never got caught. When I explained that to him, his response was, "I read a letter that you wrote to one of your ex-boyfriends telling him that you were going to miss him, and I want to break up with you." I tried to explain I only wrote that letter because I was moving. I wasn't trying to get back together with him. But nothing was going to convince Johnny that I was telling the truth. I realize now he was probably trying to find a reason to break up with me. I asked him if he would still take me to prom because my mom had already spent a lot of money on a dress, shoes, jewelry, etc. As heartbroken as I was because of his breaking up with me, I was more worried about my mom being hurt for me. "Just get me in the door, and then I promise you can go hang out with your friends. I won't even talk to you." But his answer was still no.

Finally, I convinced him to at least come to my house and pretend he was there to pick me up for prom. He then could drop me off at my best friend April's house. I was so nervous and sad getting ready that night. It's hard to put your makeup on when the only thing you want to do is burst into tears, but I couldn't let my mom find out. I had to keep it together and not cry. In fact, not only could I not cry, but I had to pretend I was happy and excited too. So that's what I did. I got dressed up in my prom dress, smiled while my mom took pictures of us in the living room, and sat quietly as Johnny drove me to my friend's house and dropped me off.

I cried tear after tear as my friend April took all the bobby pins and barrettes out of my hair. I didn't think I was ever going to stop crying. That was the first time I had ever had my heart broken like that. Once my hair was down, I redid my makeup and April and I snuck out her window. We met boys in the park, and it was there that I took my first hit of acid. I stepped out of the window a different person that night. I was going to prove to the world that I was worth it, no matter what I had to do.

I dreaded the next week at school, hearing all the prom stories, seeing all of the pictures; I just wanted to stay at home in bed. But I went and obviously survived. They showed the prom video in study hall, and there was my boyfriend dancing to "Lady in Red" with a girl who was in a red dress. I remember wanting to throw up. Besides, why did they have to use that song anyway? I really liked that song, and it totally ruined it for me. Oh, well who cares anyway . . . right? I mean I will never, ever talk to him again!

That is what I *wanted* to do—make him suffer by not even acknowledging him. I wanted to prove to him that I didn't need him then, and I definitely didn't need him now. That lasted for a few weeks, until one day he came up to me when I was hanging out with some friends. "Hey, Nanci, I'm heading home after lunch today. If you skip school, maybe you can stop by and hang out." Part of me wanted to say, "Are you crazy? You broke my heart, and now you want me to go hang out with you?" But I didn't want him to have a clue of how much he hurt me, so I said, "Ok, maybe," and walked off to my next class. The next two hours, I did everything I could to find a ride to his house. All I kept thinking was . . . maybe he really wants to get back together, maybe he felt bad for hurting me and wants to tell me how sorry he is and that he'll never do it again. That's what I was hoping for anyway. I finally found a ride with some of my sister's friends who were leaving school early. I hid in the back of the car to get past the security guard in the school parking lot and had them drop me off at Johnny's apartment. I was nervous to see him again. That should have been my first clue in knowing I probably wasn't making the best decision. But I wanted to feel better. I wanted him to like me and somehow undo the hurt he caused me. I wanted to give him another chance to love me the way I thought he did. I didn't want to give up on what my mind had created.

So there I was, fifteen years old, skipping school to see the person who had only weeks before broken my heart. The second he smiled at me, I believed things would be better. So that very day after hearing him say, "Nanci, I think you're ready," not only did I give my broken heart back to him, but I gave him my innocence as well. Tears stung my eyes and all I could think of was how heartbroken my parents would be. He dropped me off at my house later that evening. On the way home he said to me confidently, "You will probably fall in love with me now." He then hugged me and said, "I'll see you around."

Chapter 4

That summer I moved to Durant, Johnny joined the Navy, and we wrote back and forth for a while. One of the cards he sent to me said, "I joined the Navy to see the world, and now I'd give the world to see you." I read that wishing it was true, but I knew it wasn't. It was like it had finally dawned on me—love isn't at all what I pictured it to be. Those unrealistic expectations are just that—UNREALISTIC. It was almost like a revelation to me. No longer was I that innocent little girl that was boy crazy and looking for love. I didn't really care anymore. I didn't need anyone to love. I think that is part of what happens when you lose your innocence. You lose the happiness and joy you once had. You start feeling like you never really deserved it in the first place. It's obvious to me now what was happening in my life then. I was starting to question who

I was and where I belonged. I started going to summer school at Durant High School to catch up on some of my classes, and as time went by, Johnny and I both moved on—Johnny, with a career in the Navy and me with a determination to never get hurt.

Don't get me wrong, I was excited about being the new girl in a new town. It reminded me of a country song about a city girl falling in love with a country boy while working at the local diner. It sounds silly now, but I pictured that in my mind. The first time my mom and I visited Durant and ate at the Pizza Hut down the street from where we would live, I pictured myself in that song!

That country song did come true for me in a sense. The city girl started dating a country boy she had met in summer school. His name was Dalton, and he was definitely a country boy with a bright smile and a gorgeous singing voice. He was charming. I knew by the second or third day of summer school, Dalton liked me, and when he asked me out, I couldn't say no. I remember one of the first dates we went on. His aunt lived on a houseboat on Lake Texoma, so he invited me to go out there with him. My mom liked Dalton after she met him and agreed to let me go. So we went, met his aunt, and then she left. Dalton and I had the houseboat to ourselves. He offered me a wine cooler and I accepted. I had not done much drinking before, but I enjoyed hanging out with Dalton. As the night went on, I got a taste of freedom that was totally new to me. And for the first time since moving to Durant, I felt accepted.

Dalton and I dated throughout the summer and I began drinking more and more. Starting my sophomore year at Durant High School was a little easier than I thought because I had made a few friends in summer school, and Dalton and I were still together. However, I quickly realized after school started that no matter how much I felt at home, I was still the new girl to everyone else.

It didn't take long for the rumors to start. I couldn't believe some of the things people were saying about me. One rumor I heard was that I slept with the whole Southeastern College football team. I didn't even know Southeastern had a football team! On several occasions, I would be walking down the hall, and hear someone say, "There's the new bitch" or "Here comes 'Raccoon Eyes.'" People would bump into me in the stairwell, almost knocking me over, and never say one word to me. I had no idea what I was up against. I was thinking, "I don't even know these people, and I know they don't know me. Why does everyone hate me?"

I would hang out with Dalton and his friends on the weekend. We would go to Bill's gas station where everyone hung out on Main Street. But as soon as Dalton's ex-girlfriend found out about me, she would follow me around, trying to fight me. One night, we were in the car at a stop light when she ran into the street, opened the door and tried to pull me out! It was insane. I had never been so hated in my life, and I had no idea what I had done wrong. But honestly, I didn't really have anyone to turn to. I loved my parents, but I was fifteen, the age where peer acceptance is what I wanted the most. All of my good friends were back in Mustang, even my sister and brother were in Mustang, so here I was alone and the only one that I had to turn to was Dalton. He seemed to love me and care about me, and I trusted him. As long as I had him, I would be fine.

My mom was starting to wonder what I was up to and started questioning our relationship more. I had become somewhat withdrawn, spending most of my time with Dalton. I think she knew I was headed down the wrong path. Once again, I had started skipping school and stopped coming home when I was supposed to. My parents tried to talk to me about my behavior, but I protested and told them I was just fine. I didn't need their help. All I wanted was the freedom to do as I pleased without anyone's input.

Once my grades started to drop, my mom and dad scheduled a meeting with my principal to see what we could do to bring my grades up. Everyone was really concerned during this meeting, trying to understand what I was going through. My response was, well if my mom and dad would just buy me a pink pager, everything would be fine. I know that sounds childish and I'm definitely showing my age with the whole pager thing, but I felt like I deserved what I wanted!

My parents still give me a hard time about the "pink pager." I wish that was all I needed to solve my problems.

I didn't get a pager and, after many fights with my parents, I decided I would go live with Dalton's cousin, Kyla. Her parents let her do whatever she wanted, and I would be so much happier over there. So I left, leaving everything behind. I didn't realize until later that when I left home, my parents kept my turtle lamp lit in my bedroom window every night. They wanted me to know when I drove by they were thinking of me and wanting me to remember where home was. I stayed with Dalton's cousin, Kyla, for a couple of weeks. Until the night we went to the party at the mobile home, and Kyla and Dalton's ex-girlfriend tried to fight me. I knew after that night, my life was getting out of control, but I was driven by my insecurities, and Dalton was all I had.

Not only had Dalton and I been drinking together, but we had started using drugs. I had tried cocaine before with another group, but Dalton and I were getting more into crank. It was very easy for us to get drugs as his family had connections. In fact, one time my mom and dad had actually questioned me about drug use. I denied it, saying I had never done anything but smoke pot. They insisted that I take a drug test, and I finally gave in. I didn't know this then, but my dad turned that test into the hospital under his name to protect me. It tested positive for cocaine and methamphetamines. Dalton used to leave dope on my window sill before I left home. It didn't help later on that my mom found a note in my pocket from Dalton. It said, "How did you like that stuff we did this morning? I'm getting an eight ball after school." My mom was catching on, and I was quickly running out of lies.

Chapter 5

I knew my parents were worried about me. My mom was constantly writing me little notes to tell me she loved me and she was praying for me. She would drive around looking for me all night. She would put newspaper articles on my bed about drug addiction. My mom covered me in prayer every second of the day. This is why later when she told me about the dream she had, it broke my heart. She told me, in the dream, I was calling for her and she couldn't find me. It made sense when we realized it was on the very night I was walking down the gravel road praying for her to find me. My mom's heart was broken for her daughter and, though I knew that, I couldn't walk away.

I started staying with another friend, Shannon. Shannon and her boyfriend shared a house together, and she told me I could stay with them for a while if I needed to. It was around Christmas time, and I knew my family missed me. So I decided to go home for a few days and spend Christmas with them. My grandparents were there, and I didn't want them to worry about me. So I went home, opened my presents with my family, and later that night snuck out the window and was gone again. My mom told me later that Granddad stayed home from church the next day waiting for me to come back.

I didn't come back the next morning but did a few days later to get my Christmas presents. I packed a small bag and went back to Shannon's house. That next night, we were all partying and drinking when we heard a car door. I looked outside and it was my dad. I thought he was coming to beg me to come back home and tell me how much he loved me. So I went outside to meet him. In his hands were two or three trash bags with all my stuff in them. I can't remember the exact words he said, but I'm sure it was something like, "Nanci, we love you, but this is the choice you've made." I couldn't walk away from the stronghold of addiction that I had found. So that night when my dad dropped my bags of clothes off, I knew the choice I had made was big.

The next day I tried to go home and get the rest of my stuff, but the doors were locked. I tried my key, but it no longer worked. My mom's car was in the driveway, so I knew she was home. After I rang the doorbell several times, I went through the side gate to the back window. I saw my mom sitting there, playing solitaire in the living room. I knocked and knocked. I knew she heard me, but she never looked up. I was upset that she wouldn't even acknowledge me, but I was also sad for her. How broken my family had become.

I know this was all just as hard on my dad because he and I were a lot a like. We had the same interests—reading, writing, history and poetry. We used to reenact the Civil War together and had a lot of fun times. But my dad knew there was nothing that could be done until I was willing to recognize I had a problem. He knew I was lost, and he knew that no matter what he and my mom did, it wouldn't matter unless I was willing to help myself. They had done all they could do. They had tried to protect me and keep me safe, but they knew by my behavior and drug use, that I was my own worst enemy. And I knew that until I got my life straightened out, I couldn't return home and try to make it work.

So after staying with Shannon for a while, Dalton's dad got a house in Caddo, and Dalton asked me to go out there and stay with him. I agreed and moved to Caddo with Dalton. The house they were staying in was an old house full of nothing but unpacked boxes. Dalton's dad and his stepmom really had no intentions of settling in. They weren't there to build a happy home; they were there for their primary focus—to use drugs.

We were all doped out. I remember sitting on the couch and seeing a family picture of Dalton's stepmom and her daughter. I don't think his stepmom was using at the time the picture was taken because she looked happy and healthy. Her face was full and bright. I looked at the portrait for a minute, and then looked over to the other side of the room where she was standing. It made me sick to my stomach. It was like looking at a skeleton with skin. She was so thin her cheek bones were protruding and her eyes were dark and sunken. It looked as though her drug use had eaten her up from the inside out. It was a sickening reality of what drugs would do to your body.

Dalton's dad and stepmom didn't just snort dope like Dalton and I did—they shot up. So there would be times when I would have to help his dad tie the rubber around his arm to get a bump. One time we were standing in the kitchen. I was already high and was helping his dad get the dope ready to inject. I tied the rubber around his arm. He shot up, looked me in the face, and said, "Nanci, watch my eyes grow." Immediately, his pupils dilated. They turned black to the point where I couldn't tell what color his eyes were. He was like a prisoner trying to find life in everything but himself. It was sad and disturbing at the same time.

After not eating for a week and seeing everything I had seen, I was drained. Emotionally, mentally, and physically my body was drained. My mind was full of fear. "Is this what I was going to become? Is this what I had to look forward to in life?" My heart sank, and I knew it was time for me to go home. I couldn't live like this anymore. The dark, negative surroundings were overwhelming, and there was no joy in my life. I had to borrow money from Dalton's dad to go to the dollar store and buy a pair of underwear because I didn't have any. I had nothing. There were times that his dad would try to make me eat, but I couldn't. The thought of food made me sick, and my body was showing it. I went from a size two in jeans down to a double zero. I was so weak and tired, and all I could think about was being at home with my family. I wanted my sweet mom and dad in their happy home. I wanted my room with fresh clothes and all my belongings. I wanted to be with my brother and sister and my sweet little niece. I longed for the safety of my parents and their protection. I wanted to be there that second.

My mind went back to a time when my brother was in town and he came to Dalton's mom's house to see me. I answered the door in a Miller Light shirt and boxer shorts. These were the words my brother said to me, "Nance, I love you, but I miss the real Nanci. Let me know when the real Nanci comes back." That day, at that moment, I was too stubborn to respond. But now, in the midst of the hurt of addiction, I wanted the real

Nanci back too, more than anything. I didn't want to be who I had become anymore.

With tear-filled eyes and sorrow in my heart, I called my mom the next day and told her I wanted to come home. I told her how sorry I was and how I wanted to be better. My mom agreed to let me come home. The next morning she picked me up and brought me home. I was tired of the life I was living and was truly ready to get my life back. I was ready for a fresh new start—I was ready to go back to the house with the light on.

Love my big sister, Amarillo, Texas, 1982

At peace in my mother's arms, Amarillo, Texas, 1983

The Cosby Trio in Mustang, Oklahoma, Easter, 1988

Family picture at the Foster Family Reunion, Lake Murray, 1992

Mom and me, beginning the difficult years,
Durant, Oklahoma, 1997

During the drug use, Madill,
Oklahoma, 1998

My car after the wreck, 1998

Close up of my car, 1998

My sweet Kaylan Hope at her baby shower,
Tulsa, Oklahoma, 2000

My little "Addie Bug," Addison Tate Reed,
Tulsa, Oklahoma 2003

Kaylan Hope and Addison Tate,
Tulsa, Oklahoma, 2003

Oil painting reflecting my testimony, II Corinthians 5:17,
Tulsa, Oklahoma, 2003

Kaylan Hope's Kindergarten Graduation,
Mustang, Oklahoma, 2007

Robbie and me at the beginning of our relationship, 2008

Mom, dad, and siblings at our wedding, Saint Stephens
United Methodist Church, Amarillo, Texas, July 11, 2009

Our first Christmas picture as a blended family,
Mustang, Oklahoma 2009

Chapter 6

Dalton and I stopped seeing each other not long after I moved back home. Not only had I found out that he had cheated on me more than once, but I was starting to realize how unhealthy our relationship was. The drugs we did ruined any "good" we might have had together. I got to the point where I didn't even want to see or speak to him anymore. There was too much darkness attached to that relationship, and I was ready to move on.

Being back at home wasn't that bad. I enrolled at Vision Academy, the alternative school, and started going to class, trying to make up my grades. Some of my friends went there too, so it was good to get to hang out with them again. My two best friends Leigh and Brent, were glad to have me back. Aside from Dalton, they had been my biggest support system. Leigh and I had met the first day of Durant High School, when we were both looking for the cafeteria. It had been her first day too. She quickly became my new best friend. Brent was the same way. During the time I decided to leave home, he and I hung out at Taco Casa and shared nachos together. He was like a brother to me. We all did our fair amount of partying together, but they were different from my other friends. They truly cared about who I was. I had other friends in Durant that were the same way. So even through all the struggles of addiction, I managed to make some really good friends.

Being back home felt right. I still struggled with my meth addiction but soon took up alcohol as my next drug of choice, and before I knew it I was back to drinking all the time. I felt like I was a little more in control of my addiction and got to the point where I could take it or leave it. I guess in my mind I felt like, because alcohol wasn't as bad as drugs, I was better off! That was my thinking.

I didn't realize I was trading one addiction for another. I was just trying to get through life, trying to find who I was. It never dawned on me those addictions were shaping who and what was to come. My mom once described depression as trying to read a book so close to your face you can't see what's written on the page or anything beyond or around the book. You can't see the family and friends you are hurting. All you see is what's right in front of you, and it is distorted, at best! I believe that about addiction as well. I couldn't see the destructive things I was doing to myself or my family. I only saw what was right in front of me. And what was right in front of me was my desire to escape through my addiction.

I still believed in God. I loved God. In fact, I swore that my sister and I were the only ones who talked about God when we were stoned or drinking together. I would argue with anyone who didn't believe in Him. I hated when people questioned my beliefs and doubted Christ's existence. It was never a question of whether or not I believed in Him, I just struggled with accepting that He believed in me. So it was easier to be high or drunk and have an excuse of why my life was a mess than to try to live a normal life and mess up anyway. Alcohol became my scapegoat. I had to have an excuse as to why my life was the way it was.

Not long after moving back home, my dad accepted the position of Associate Pastor at First United Methodist Church, Tulsa, Oklahoma. My mom was in the process of becoming a Licensed Professional Counselor and was employed in Madill, Oklahoma, where her employer was paying for her supervision. As a result, the plan was for my mom and I to move to Madill so she could finish her supervision within the year and then we would join my dad in Tulsa.

We made the move, and I enrolled in alternative night school at Madill High and started working with my mom during the day. I was the receptionist at a nursing home management center that managed six nursing homes, and my mom was the Clinical Director and supervised the clinicians providing counseling in the nursing homes.

Mom helped me buy a car so I still got to see my friends, Leigh and Brent, from Durant. All in all, the move wasn't that bad. She let me have the master bedroom of our rent house and took me to buy yellow towels and rugs for my bathroom. I was excited about having a new house, and it was neat getting to live with her. It was great getting to spend that time with her as we started this new period of our lives.

I was still going back and forth to Durant to see my friends. And unfortunately still getting into trouble. My mom took me to an AA meeting once in Ardmore, trying to help me. I left there thinking—I do not belong in an AA group with those people! She also made arrangements for me to go to counseling. I went a couple of times, but to this day, I could not tell you what I learned or what we talked about.

My addiction was probably harder on my mom than anyone. Her granddad had been an alcoholic most of his life, and her younger brother was a recovering alcoholic and addict. She had already been down this road more than once. I'm sure it was hard for her without my dad there to help. She did her best to take care of me, but she knew I was living in a world of self-destruction. She continued to pray for me that no matter what I went through God would protect me and keep me safe.

I came home one day with two black eyes, stitches on my cheek, and looked pretty miserable. I had been in a fight the night before and had to go to the hospital for stitches. I thought my mom would feel sorry for me, but it's hard to feel sorry for someone who allows these kinds of things to happen to her. I'm sure her heart did hurt for me, but she knew she couldn't help me.

Time after time, my mom could see the effects of my addiction. She coped by trying to live one day at a time and when that was too much, it was one hour at a time. She clung to the verse: "Train up a child in the way he should go, and when he is old he will not turn from it" (Proverbs 22). Her prayer for me was always this: "No matter what path Nanci takes in life, please let it end at the cross." She had to surrender her motherly expectations and trust God with my life. She knew He would be with me every step of the way, even though she didn't know where I was headed.

One positive thing in my life was this—I actually liked going to night school. I began to make good grades and pass my classes. My classes were on a computer program, so I would have to take a final test on each class to complete that subject. It was a "work at your own pace" curriculum, so there wasn't a lot of pressure involved. I knew if I wanted to graduate, I had better stay focused. I liked our instructor, Mr. Carter, too. He was an older man and had been retired for years, but I thought he was pretty cool. For once, I felt like I had a chance to do something with my life, and I was eager to see it through.

Chapter 7

The following October, my mom and dad planned a trip to Ireland with friends. They had always wanted to visit Ireland, so I was so happy they had the chance to go. The morning they left, my sister and I met them to say our goodbyes. Carmen and I would be staying at the house by ourselves, and I knew my mom and dad would worry about us. In fact, before they left, my mom said, "Nance, please, whatever you do, just stay home while we're gone. I'd feel better knowing that you weren't out with friends, so please just stay home." I promised her that day that I would. I didn't want her to worry about me. After all, there was nothing to worry about!

We had a good time together as a family that morning. We laughed together, cried together, and finally gave hugs and said our goodbyes. We waved goodbye as my parents drove away, none of us knowing that by the time they came back, our lives would be forever changed.

I kept the promise I made to my mom the first couple of nights by staying home. But the weekend was fast approaching, and I knew everyone would be ready to party. I didn't want to miss out on anything, so I agreed to pick up my friend Shaylee and head to the club that following Thursday night.

After picking up Shaylee, we headed to the Roadhouse in Durant to meet our friends. We probably stopped by a few places before to hang out, but I honestly don't remember. My best friend Leigh, Shaylee's cousin, was grounded that night so she couldn't go with us. Shaylee and I met my sister and my friend Brent at the club. Several of our other friends were there as well, including Chris, the guy I was dating at the time. We closed the club down that night and, as we started to leave, I told Shaylee, "I think I just want to stay at Chris' house tonight so we don't have to drive all the way back to Madill." Durant was around twenty to thirty minutes from Madill, and I was tired, so I really didn't want to make that drive. Shaylee didn't want to stay at Chris', so I agreed to drive us back to my house.

As we were leaving, I said to myself, "I think I'll drive home the back way to avoid traffic and the police." So on we went curving through the roads of the Washita Valley that separated Durant from Madill. I didn't feel extremely drunk that night, but I knew I had consumed quite a bit of alcohol and I was exhausted.

I don't remember much about the drive home other than Shaylee screaming, "Nanci . . . lights!" As I looked ahead of me, it was too late. My car hit the left front side of a truck that was coming from the other direction. I don't remember the impact of the crash at all. All I remember is being in front of a house and hearing voices muffled in the background. At one point I heard someone say, "That's my dad! Is he going to be ok?" Shaylee was screaming in the passenger seat and when I tried to help her, my body felt broken. I couldn't move. I was conscious, but I could not move my body. I couldn't help Shaylee or myself. I sat there in my car paralyzed, not sure what just happened. The paramedics arrived, along with a crew to open my car with what they called "the jaws of life." When they were trying to get me out of the car, I realized I was hurt pretty badly. My left ankle was pinned under the clutch, and the lower part of my body was in extreme pain, especially when they were trying to get me out of the car. I don't remember the ambulance ride to Durant that night. I just remember getting to the hospital and seeing my sister. I was so happy to see her, but I was scared of how hurt I was. The first thing I said to my sister when I saw her was, "Carmen is everyone ok?" She had been crying and upset, but she nodded her head and said, "Yes, Nanci, everything is fine." I looked up at her, so glad she was there, and said, "Carm, I'm sicky."

I didn't know it at the time, but the ER doctors were preparing me for immediate surgery. They used some sort of a vacuum to suck out the fluids in my stomach. They gave me a blood transfusion and put me in a blow-up suit so I could be medivacked to Parkland Hospital in Dallas, Texas. With my parents in Ireland, my sister was the only family I had with me. So as I flew to Dallas in a helicopter, Carmen came in her car, driving as fast as she could. Shaylee was released with minor injuries.

When I was in the pre-operation room at Parkland, my Aunt Sharla, who lived in Midlothian, was there to meet me. She stayed in the emergency room with me while they finished prepping me for surgery. My ankle was completely crushed, my pelvic bone was broken, and the doctors were worried about the internal damages I might have due to the pelvic injury. I was in so much pain and probably wasn't thinking clearly, but I remember feeling bad for cussing with my aunt in the room!

I think it was in this room that I got to talk to my parents for the first time. Their travel agent had been contacted while they were in Ireland and had been told that Stan and Susan Cosby's daughter had been in a car accident. They didn't elaborate on the details, or even tell my parents if I was ok. But my parents were somehow able to call the hospital and find where I was. My mom said as she waited for someone to answer, the song from *American Tail* was playing on the phone, *"Somewhere out there, someone's saying a prayer, that we'll find one another, in that big somewhere out there."* And then she heard my voice.

I don't remember the conversation. I only remember waking up from surgery to all of my family there. My brother had asked for an advance on his paycheck so he could have the money to fly to Dallas. Meemee and Granddad and Uncle Tom had also come down. What a blessing it was to be surrounded by family.

The first thing I did when I saw my mom was ask her if everyone was ok. That's when I found out what really happened. She told me everything: "No, Nance, the man in the other car didn't make it." Her face and tears had already answered my question before she spoke those words. When I had asked Carmen the same question before surgery she had been instructed to not give me any details about the wreck. The doctors had told her they needed me to be as strong as I could before my surgeries. I had a feeling when I talked to Carmen before that something had happened. I wasn't sure what, but I knew it wasn't good. So when my mom told me everything, I was heartbroken.

I had so many questions, but who do you ask? I'm the one that was there that night. I'm the one that should have already known. The article in the Durant paper read something like this: "Mr. Larry Nelson, 62 years old, was pronounced dead at the scene. The car accident happened at 3:52 a.m., on a highway in Little City, just outside of Madill. Mr. Nelson was coming home from a fishing trip with his family who was following in the car behind, when he was hit by a drunk driver, 18-year-old Nanci Cosby of Madill. Nanci Cosby was medivacked to Parkland Hospital in Dallas with severe injuries to ankle and pelvis." It seemed so surreal to me at times. Yes, I remembered the wreck, but what happened before and after was somewhat of a blur to me.

Chapter 8

I was in the hospital for two weeks and finally got to go home. My mom took me to see my car on the way home from the hospital. I couldn't believe what I saw. The left front was completely caved in and the glass shattered, but not a piece of the front windshield had broken out. It was eerie to think I had been sitting in the driver's seat. It was truly a miracle that I survived, and I knew, without a doubt, God had protected me.

The support I received from friends and family was unbelievable. I received so many cards and letters of encouragement. People from all the different churches where my dad had served were praying for me. I was covered in prayer, and it helped me through some of the hardest days during my recovery.

The healing process seemed long. I had to be on crutches for the three months due to the injuries. I had eight screws and a plate in my left ankle and three nine-inch screws in my pelvis. My mom drove me back and forth to Dallas to see my doctors. Since my ankle had been in a cast since the surgery, I had no idea what to expect when it was time to remove the cast. My mom held my hand as they cut the cast off, and when I saw my ankle for the first time, I broke down.

I expected my ankle to be bruised and swollen, but I was not prepared for it to be as wide as my calf. There was a row of black stitches running down both sides, marking the place where they put the plate and screws in. I felt like I was Frankenstein with all the stitches—there were too many to count! I remember thinking, "My leg is so ugly." I looked at my mom and said, "Mom, it's never going to be the same, is it?" She was crying too as she walked over to me, gave me a hug, and said, "Nanci, let's just be thankful you still have it." My mom shared with me later that she believed those scars would always be a precious reminder of God's mercy in keeping her sweet girl safe!

Chapter 9

Weeks had gone by, and I hadn't heard from the Nelson family or the police, for that matter. I didn't know what to expect as far as punishment was concerned. I remember thinking to myself, "Please put me in jail. I don't deserve anything but the worst. Please do whatever you think it takes." I also wrote a letter to the family, trying to express in words how sorry I was for what happened. Tears flowed down my face as I wrote that letter. In a lot of ways that was probably the first time I had actually come to terms with what happened.

When I was finally able to go back to work, a highway patrol officer came to visit me and took a written report of my side of the story. He wasn't mean or accusatory; he simply asked questions. Sitting in that conference room, I told him everything I remembered about that night. How I had been drinking at the club with friends, how I tried to take the back way home to avoid traffic, how I heard Shaylee scream, "Lights!" and everything that happened after that. When I finished giving my report, I told the officer that I was willing to do whatever it took to face my punishment, that I was so sorry it happened and that I would do anything to change the outcome of that night. The officer shook my hand and said he'd be in contact with me. He told me that he might recommend that I share my story in local high schools. He thanked me for my time and was out the door.

I never heard from that officer again, but I did receive a letter in the mail from Mr. Nelson's family. The letter was in a blue envelope with pink writing; I was so nervous to open that letter. I knew I deserved to be hated, but I didn't want to be. I wanted them to know my heart and know that I would never ever purposely hurt anyone. That's what I tried to say in the letter I wrote them. I tried to show them how sorry I was. I had waited for weeks to hear from them. But now that I had the letter in my hands, I was afraid to open it.

I read the letter they wrote to me over and over. It wasn't a letter of accusation or hate; it was a letter of love, telling me they believed God had given me a second chance and they didn't want me to waste it. I couldn't believe it! I didn't think I could have been that forgiving had the roles been reversed. How blessed I was to be on the receiving end of God's grace and their forgiveness. I knew God had given me a second chance, and I wanted to make the very best of it.

When I started getting better, I wanted to start hanging out with my friends again. I obviously didn't have a car and didn't plan on driving anytime soon, so my friends would come pick me up to hang out. The more I got out, the more I wanted my old life back. I knew I shouldn't start drinking again, but it didn't take long for me to be right back in the middle of it like I was once before. I started going to parties when I was still on crutches. Once at a party someone said to me, "Don't you feel bad drinking after your car wreck?" The truth was I did feel bad, but getting away from that lifestyle wasn't as easy as one might think.

So I continued to party and live just like I did before the wreck. No direction, no responsibility, just selfish me doing as I pleased. But one night when I was out with my friends Leigh and Mark, something changed. We were backroading in Durant, all of a sudden, I said to them, "I'm moving to Tulsa with my dad." I don't know where that came from. I had never even thought about moving to Tulsa, but as those words came out of my mouth, I knew that was what I was going to do. As the radio played the song from Armageddon, "Leaving on a Jet Plane," I knew I was leaving. My friends and I drank our beer and cried together that night. They knew I was ready.

That next week, I talked to my mom and dad about it, and they all agreed it would be the best thing for me. I had already finished my school and planned to walk across stage that next spring to graduate. I had no reason to stay in Madill, and honestly I was ready to get out. I packed my things, said goodbye to my mom and friends, and headed to Tulsa with my dad.

It was on that drive to Tulsa that my dad and I really had a heart-to-heart talk. My dad is a wise man and has a way of saying things that go straight to the heart. Just ask my brother and sister! I shared my heart with my dad on that trip. I'll never forget that he said, "Nanci, you can keep running all you want . . . but one of these days God is going to get a hold of you and you'll never turn back." I'm not sure I said a whole lot after that. I probably didn't admit it at the time, but I believed him and knew he was right.

Chapter 10

Those next few months with my dad were very refreshing for me. I was away from all the distractions, and I didn't have any new friends in Tulsa. My brother lived there so I got to see him some. Other than that, it was me and my dad. We worked out at the church gym together. We read the same books and shared scriptures with one another. He would buy all my favorite kinds of food, and he and I would eat dinner together. It was a very special time for my dad and me. We got to spend quality time that was much needed, and it felt good. I'm sure it was a relief to my mom, too. She didn't have to worry about me anymore, and she deserved some peace.

Tulsa was a great place to live. One of my dad's friends got me a receptionist job at an architectural firm. I started working full time and really enjoyed it. I went back to Madill that next spring to graduate and walk across the stage. It was a great feeling. It was good to see my friends and hang out with them, but once it was time for me to head back to Tulsa, I was more than ready. I had learned to love my quiet life, and I was ready to get back to it.

Even though I didn't really have any friends in Tulsa, I did go out on a date with one of the guys I met at church. He was so sweet and I really liked him, but after hanging out with him and his friends, I felt like I was too different. I was used to hanging out with party people, not churchy people, so I felt out of place. I never heard from him after our first date. He probably thought I was like some biker babe or something. Compared to him, I probably was! It was hard for me because I felt like I wasn't good enough, but I still hoped that one day I would find the right person!

I did miss having friends to talk to, but I was doing so well. I stayed motivated and felt very content. One day, my dad told me that a lady at the church was wondering if I could call and talk to her friend's daughter. The daughter was really struggling with drugs and alcohol and was apparently in a bad relationship. So I called, and Lacy and I started talking on the phone. I enjoyed having someone to visit with.

We started hanging out more and more and had a lot of fun together. I really liked her mom and dad and would stay over there at their house quite a bit. One night, we went to one of her friend's house, and they were drinking wine. I thought I was strong enough at that point to be able to drink a little. Surely it wouldn't hurt to have a few glasses of wine. I was fine that night, but the more I hung out with her, the more I started to drink.

Through Lacy, I made some new friends. It was good to have people to spend time with. I still went to church and spent time with my dad, but I slowly started to slip back into my old habits. The book, "My Addiction," was back in my face, and that's all I was starting to focus on. I wanted to be free from it. I wanted to live righteously, but I couldn't see past it. I continued with that book in my face and walked blindly back into the life I had left behind in Durant.

I started going out to clubs with my friends, drinking my life and dreams away like I had always done. When you choose a life of addiction, things start falling apart, unraveling at the seams. Addiction was a path of destruction all too familiar. No matter where I went, regardless of whom I was with, I would find myself right back in the middle of it. Every turn I took seemed to be the wrong one, and I followed along, not knowing any different, until hope was revealed to me in a mighty way.

Chapter 11

Meeting Lacy allowed me to meet a lot more people in Tulsa. And though some of those relationships weren't the best, I did meet some really good people and still consider them to be my good friends today—Luke and Christine and Luke's sister, Anna. Luke and Christine were married and had their own house! I found their life intriguing as they both had a relationship with Christ and talked openly about God. Anna was my party girl! Every weekend she and I would brave the clubs together, waiting in line outside, freezing cold in our miniskirts. I also met Lacy's ex-boyfriend, Josh. We didn't really like each other at first but soon became good friends. And then there was Marlee. We both had been through a lot and had a strange kind of understanding of each other. She had lost her mom to an eating disorder so we were both learning to live with grief.

With all my club-hopping and party-going, I did start dating again. I made a few mistakes in that process but ended up seriously dating a guy named Kyle. Kyle liked to drink too, so that was probably the main thing we had in common. We drank a lot together. It was very strange the night I met him. I was at a party and, when he walked in, our eyes met, and I knew we would be together. We told everyone at that party that we were going to get married, and after that night we spent every day together.

Because drinking was such a big part of our relationship, there were a lot of issues. We would go through a case of beer every night, twelve beers apiece. We fought a lot, and I knew we were more party buddies than boyfriend and girlfriend. I stayed at Kyle's house more than I stayed at home, and, in a way, we were playing house.

One weekend my best friend Brent came down to visit. We were planning to go out that night, so my sister Carmen and I went to Brent's hotel room to have a few beers first. It was strange because I drank two beers and felt like I needed to throw up. Brent said, "Nance, what is wrong with you? I know you can drink more than two beers." I agreed, but couldn't bring myself to take another drink.

My sister said, "Maybe you're pregnant." I thought there was no way, but I couldn't even recall when I had my last period. We went to Walgreens to buy a test; I took the test and it was negative. "Party on," I thought, and didn't think another thing about it.

Another week went by and I still hadn't started. I thought maybe I should buy another test just in case and took it that night when I was at Kyle's house. This time it came out positive. Kyle was ironing his pants when I came out of the bathroom. By the look on my face, I think he knew. He dropped the iron on the floor. He couldn't believe it either. I was pregnant!

My sister went to my first doctor's appointment with me. She was so supportive. I was scared to death to tell my parents. I was afraid of disappointing them again. But Carmen and I agreed that I had to tell them. A few nights later my sister and I had a glass of wine together, knowing it would be our last, and then drove to my parent's house. I sat on the edge of my bed with Carmen by my side and I broke down. I told my mom and she cried too but wrapped her arms around me and told me it was going to be ok. Wow, what a great mom! My dad was also very supportive and chose to love me anyway. Despite all I had put my family through, my parents stood by my side. I had no idea at that moment how much I would need them the next nine months.

It really didn't take that long for the excitement to kick in. Of course, it was hard to wrap my mind around the fact that I was going to be a mommy! Two months after I found out I was pregnant, I decided it was best for Kyle and me to break up. I knew I had to take care of myself, and spending time in a party environment was not going to be healthy for me or the baby. It was hard letting go of that relationship. I was sad that I would not be marrying the father of my child, but I also knew that Kyle and I were not meant for each other, and I had to follow through with that decision.

My mom and dad truly became my life partners during my pregnancy. I was extremely sick through the first two trimesters and could barely gain weight. After one of my ultrasounds, the doctor said, "Miss Cosby, your baby's measurements are not where they should be. We really need you to try to gain as much weight as possible even if you have to drink ensure and live on ice cream sundaes. It's imperative that you start gaining weight."

I left that doctor's office in tears. I never even imagined something going wrong with my pregnancy. I just assumed I would have a happy, healthy baby. Worried, I called my mom crying, and she comforted me as always.

I did the best I could to gain weight. I craved Mexican food, so my parents and I would go to dinner together quite often. I would eat as much as I could and beg my dad to drive fast on the way home because I knew I would be hugging the toilet soon!

At work, I would have to put people on hold so I could run to the bathroom to empty my stomach and then get back to my desk to transfer the call. Pregnancy was definitely life changing for me. It was also a time of complete surrender to God. Every thought of my precious baby brought me closer to

God, and I began to feel Him in a way I had never experienced Him before. He was becoming *my* God . . . not just my mom and dad's God.

God was also working on healing the relationship with my parents. After my teenage years, there were definitely some unresolved issues. Trust had been broken, so I'm sure my parents were fearful I might return to my old lifestyle, but they didn't live in that fear. They took me in with open arms and spent every second they could with me. We went to dinner and movies together. We even went to a Michael W. Smith concert together. They became my very best friends. One of my best memories of being pregnant was the 4th of July before Kaylan was born. She was born exactly a month after the holiday, so I was big and pregnant. My mom had made an awesome meal, and the family was all together. I remember putting little American flag toothpicks in the deviled eggs and thinking, "I am one lucky girl." Everything in my life seemed to be coming together, and I felt peaceful.

Needless to say, when Kaylan came into this world, things were not so peaceful. The screws in my pelvis from the car wreck made the childbirth extremely painful. Not to mention the fact that I was in labor for twenty-six hours and could not seem to dilate. Kaylan was already passed her due date, so the night before I went into labor, my mom said, "Let's go walk this baby out." The three of us—Mom, Dad, and myself (well, four including Kaylan)—walked around LeFortune Park—almost three miles. I couldn't quite make it back to the car, so dad walked back to get the car to pick us up. During the night I woke with labor pains I had not felt before. We loaded up and went to the hospital only to be sent home later because I had not dilated. I thought to myself, the next time I go to that hospital I am coming home with a baby!

I went home and tried to get some rest. I was in so much pain, I could hardly take it, but I had made my mind up—I'm not getting sent home again. Later that day, my mom and brother and I decided to go to the mall to walk around. My poor brother—every five or ten minutes I would stop, grab his arm, and squeeze as hard as I could, until the contraction passed. People walking by probably thought we were nuts. The more we walked, the more I hurt. It took everything I had to not scream and yell right there in the middle of the mall. I finally told my mom that it was time to go back to the hospital.

When we left the mall, Dave needed to stop by the bank. A few minutes felt like forever. I wanted to scream at him when he got back in the car. We headed back up to the hospital, and this time they did not send me home.

I was finally starting to dilate, and Kaylan was on her way. The nurse broke my water, and the contractions and I worked together. Kaylan was born at 3:51 the next morning, August 4th. She struggled during the birth process and, as her heart rate dropped, the nurses had to massage the top of her head to get her heart rate back up. I was so weak, I didn't even have the energy to worry, but I know my mom was worrying enough for the both of us.

After my mom cut the umbilical cord, Kaylan was placed on my stomach, and the mother-daughter bond was immediate. In fact, it had already been well established nine months before. After they cleaned her up and got her wrapped in a blanket, they were wheeling me to another room. The nurse asked me if I wanted to hold her, but I was so weak, I replied by saying, "I can't right now, but she is sooooo cute!"

My little Kaylan Hope was finally here—the hope of my life! I knew I couldn't change my life for myself, but I was determined to change it for that little girl, and our journey together had begun.

Chapter 12

After Kaylan was born, God continued to speak to my heart in many ways. My old habits would creep in every so often, and I would start to follow those old desires, but Kaylan helped keep my life on track.

When Kaylan was eight weeks old, I started dating again. I fell for a fun, loving, caring guy named Brandon whom I eventually married. Times were not always good. We both struggled with alcohol abuse and fought many times. The first year was fine, but the second and third years were very trying. He was great with Kaylan and we were fine when we weren't drinking together, but there was a lot of internal damage done when hateful words were exchanged. We were constantly breaking up and getting back together. Two years into our relationship, I was pregnant. I would be having another baby girl that spring.

Once again, I was faced with a situation I wasn't sure I could overcome. We decided to marry in January, three months before I was due, and bought a house together. Addison Tate was born on April 6, 2003, an absolutely perfect and precious baby. Regardless of the circumstances surrounding their births, both Addison and Kaylan were and are the loves of my life, and I am blessed to be their mommy.

Having Kaylan made me appreciate so much more in life, and when Addie was born it only confirmed that God was good. I was able to be a stay-at-home mom, but finances were tight, and stress and tension seemed to consume us. Sometimes, I would go out and party just to get away as a means of coping with it all. I loved being married and I loved being a mom, but I was lonely. I had an empty place in my heart and soul, and I wasn't sure what I was looking for.

This stress took a toll on my family life. Brandon had to constantly walk on eggshells around me because there were times I just couldn't handle it. I did continue to go to school and finally graduated with an Associate's degree, which meant the world to me. But even that achievement didn't fill that void. What was I missing? Maybe I married the wrong person. Maybe I shouldn't have married at all. There were so many questions inside my head, and I was clouded by confusion.

I slowly started to close my heart to Brandon. I tried to fulfill my desires in other places and eventually with other people. Rather than listen to my heart, honor my promise to my husband and God, and act according to my morals and values, I selfishly put myself first and committed adultery.

Strangely, I felt justified in my actions. I was blinded by my sin and simply could not find my way out. One Christmas weekend, I chose to stay home while Brandon took the girls to visit his family. I sat on my kitchen floor, with my head in my hands, crying and pleading for God's mercy. I was so full of shame and guilt, I didn't think I could go on. What had I done to my family?

I finally found the courage to tell Brandon the truth. Understandably, he was brokenhearted, but he chose to forgive me and gave me a second chance. In some ways, I hoped he wouldn't. I hoped he would hate me like I hated myself, but he didn't, and we tried again.

A year later when Addison was three, I was offered a job in Oklahoma City, at First Church, as the Director of Children's Ministry. We decided as a family to move to make a fresh start. The years at First Church were amazing to me, and my walk with God deepened. I fell in love with the church and the people, and God continued to lead me closer to Him. I also became actively involved in a 12-step program called Celebrate Recovery, and, through the twelve steps, surrendered much of the guilt and shame I had bottled up.

There was still much unresolved hurt between Brandon and me. I honestly believed it would never be the same. We divorced two years later, and it was one of the hardest things I had ever experienced, but through it God taught me much about who I am and who He has called me to be. Brandon and I both determined that during the divorce process we would do everything within our power to love and cherish our sweet girls and keep their best interests at heart.

Chapter 13

Someone once said something like this: "Divorce is like a tornado that runs through your life wreaking havoc on all it touches." I couldn't agree more. Everything in my life changed, from the car I was driving to the bed in which I slept. My parents moved to Texas when my dad was appointed to a church in the Northwest Texas Conference. I resigned from my job at the church and took another job. I fell behind on my bills and could barely hold my head above water. My heart was absolutely broken for Kaylan and Addison. They didn't deserve all of these changes. They were the innocent lives that would ultimately suffer the most from this tornado called divorce.

When we began the joint custody schedule, I would lie in my bed and cry the nights I didn't have them. My house was so quiet and empty, and I was filled with desperation. I never imagined, after carrying my babies for nine months and delivering them both into this world, that I would ever have to be apart from them, especially during holidays. The fact that I would miss out on anything in their lives broke my heart in two. They were my world, and yet, I was only their part-time mom.

The grief that fills your heart after a divorce is unexplainable. It feels like someone has knocked the breath out of you, and you struggle with all your might to get it back. Those were some of the darkest days of my life. I knew I was going to have to find strength and rely on God to pull me out of this darkness. Why would I ever doubt that He would?

The healing process began, like it usually does, through many nights of tears. In the state of Oklahoma you are required by law to take a parenting class before the divorce is final. I remember thinking, "Why would I need a parenting class? I love being a mom." But this particular parenting class was one for divorced families. It was exactly what I needed. It reassured me that my girls still love both their mommy and daddy the very same and that we are still their family, even though we were no longer living in the same house. It taught me the importance of helping my kids through this transition, and how to show respect to the other parent as well.

It dawned on me one day that I have the opportunity to teach my girls that even when the world around you crumbles, you still have a heavenly Father who is holding you in His arms. God never changes. He never leaves. He is with you always. He is the only constant in our lives and in this world, and we can always rely on Him.

God started to redirect my path through this newfound strength, and He came to me in my deepest hour of need. That's just the way our awesome God works! He began to teach me and show me His way, and I began to long for Him more than anything in this world. I was constantly reminded through Celebrate Recovery that God never wastes a hurt, and He promises to use our stories for His glory. God's word was starting to bring light to my path, and I was once again filled with a hope that only God can provide. Where was God leading me and how could I fulfill His plan?

Chapter 14

It was about this time I was contacted by the Victim's Impact Panel of Oklahoma County. A lady from First Church had shared part of my story with them, and they asked if I would be willing to come and speak. The VIP is a program that is connected to the court system. Anytime someone receives a DUI or a DWI, that person is required, by law, to attend one of these classes. The class consists of a video and three speakers who share how drinking and driving has affected their lives. The panel includes an offender, a victim (a family member who has lost a loved one), and a highway patrol officer who has worked the scene of a drinking-related accident. I would speak as the offender.

They invited me to attend one of the meetings so I could get a feel for how it worked. That night, I heard a mom share the story of her daughter and how she was killed in Padre Island on spring break by a drunk driver. Amazingly, the girl was a classmate of mine at Mustang High School, a girl I knew and loved. Her story touched my heart and that night marked another turning point in my life.

When they called me and asked me to speak at my first meeting, I was extremely nervous. I had shared my testimony only once before, at a Sunday night church service, and that about did me in. My nerves were almost uncontrollable, and I'm sure I was shaking like crazy. But I knew I was being called, and I had known enough at this point that if God calls you, He will equip you, so I agreed.

As I sat in the parking lot at Brown's Driving School, I read my Bible and prayed, "Please God, I'm so nervous, calm my heart and give me strength. I don't want to go back to that night. I don't want to share my story with strangers, but I know you have ordained this. Please Lord, give me peace."

He was faithful in answering my prayer as I found the strength to walk into the room where the panel would be held. I watched the video along with all of the people in attendance.

When the time came, I shared my story with humility I had never felt before. I realized at that point I was no longer the offender, but I was an advocate for those lost lives on the video and for the victim's families who sat next to me on the panel. God had brought me here to represent the life that was cut short because of my irresponsibility and to encourage others to make the right choice.

Since that night, I have had the opportunity to share my story with thousands of people. I was even invited by the Victim's Impact Panel to speak to the junior and senior high students at Mustang High School. God took me back to the very place where my world started falling apart. It proved that God was spinning straw of my life (my past) into gold—for my good and His glory! He had reclaimed His victory in my life and in the lives of my family. What a joy it was for me to stand in that high school gymnasium and share the hope of Christ through my personal testimony. Even some of my old teachers came up and hugged me, telling me how very proud they were. What a true blessing!

Chapter 15

After agreeing to speak that first time for the VIP, God brought me one opportunity after another to share my story. I continued to work full time, raise my beautiful girls, and share my testimony every chance I was given. I also met the love of my life. We married on July 11, 2009, after many sessions of pre-marital counseling. I was extremely happy to become Mrs. Robert Johnson.

Robbie and I had both been married before, so we knew there would be challenges ahead. We were also blending families, his daughter and my two girls, so we had our work cut out for us. They say opposites attract and this was very true for Robbie and me. I was the outgoing one who never stopped talking, and Robbie was the quiet one who doesn't say much, especially when it comes to people he doesn't know.

I fell in love with this man. He was my rock on those many nights when I missed my girls as he held me, letting me cry on his shoulder. He knew my heart was breaking, and he did his best to love me through it. He was very wise, and I counted on him in countless situations, always trusting his judgment.

After we were married, I started sharing my story at more and more panels and schools. It seemed the more I shared my story, the more God spoke to my heart. I would often pray for the group I was speaking to and ask God directly what they needed to hear, "Lord, give me the words. Show me Your way." Not only did He give me the words, but He would speak to me through dreams and visions. He brought healing to my heart through writing poetry and listening to praise music.

There was one particular night when God sent me an incredible dream. It was two nights before I was scheduled to speak. I wasn't getting a good feel for what I needed to share, so I fell asleep praying about it. As I slept, God brought me a dream . . .

My husband Robbie and I were walking down the very road where my car accident happened twelve years before. Robbie wanted to see the memorial marker they had displayed in honor of Mr. Nelson. As we were walking, we noticed a snake lying there on the side of the road. We didn't think anything of it; we just kept walking. After we arrived at the memorial marker, Robbie wanted to walk further to see all the curvy roads I had driven over before the wreck. Like all of us, he thought it was odd that I would wreck on a straight road after driving through the curves. So he and I kept walking, but as we got closer to where the curvy road should have started, we stopped. A church had been built right in the middle of the road! We went inside, and I asked someone if the roads were still there behind the church. Their answer was this, "Yes, but you can no longer get to them from here." Shocked, Robbie and I turned around and started walking back.

That's when I opened my eyes and woke up with goose bumps. God had spoken to me. He had given me that dream. This is how I believe He wanted me to interpret it. "Nanci, yes, your past is still there, but I have built a sanctuary in the midst of it; a place for you to find hope and peace. Behold, I have done a new thing. You will always remember where you've been, but you will know now that I've been there too, to bring good out of evil. The snake represents that evil. It is always lurking at your doorstep, waiting to attack. But keep your eye on me, and I will lead you down right paths."

It was truly amazing. I had never heard His word so clearly. My heart was blessed to be the recipient of such a divine message. It was so reassuring to me that God was fulfilling His purpose in my life, and I felt honored.

It was not long after that when God spoke to me again. This time, I had been asked to speak to a group of sorority girls. It was exciting to have the opportunity to speak to another group of people, but once again I needed God's help on the message. "God, what do you want them to hear from my story?" "Hope" was the answer He gave me. "Well, I know it's about Hope, but what exactly does Hope mean?" Instantly, God spoke the following words to me: "Healing, Opportunity, Purpose and Excitement." One word, right after the other, an acronym for HOPE. I'm telling you to this day, if I had to sit down and think about an acronym for hope, I would have started with "happy" or something cheesy like that. But God defined my testimony in four little words. This is how it was interpreted. Healing: God brought healing to my life in many ways. Through that healing He brought Opportunity, the opportunity to share my story with other people. Through that Opportunity came Purpose. God's Purpose for my life was revealed to me, and I knew He was going to use me in many ways. And, through that Purpose came an Excitement, God-given excitement, the excitement and passion I tried so hard to find, through all sorts of avenues. The Bible tells us that God knows the desires of our hearts even more than we do. There is nothing like the excitement of living a life for Christ! Trust me—I spent many years of my life living for myself and know the damage it had caused.

As I shared that God-given acronym with the sorority group that night, I had a small anchor with me as the symbol of hope. I shared how sometimes we are called to stay ground like an anchor, in the waves of this world. I also mentioned that someday I was going to get an anchor tattoo because I loved that symbol of hope. After I finished speaking, some of the girls came up to ask questions or share stories. One of the girls showed me the anchor tattoo on her wrist. I went on and on about how cool that was and asked her what made her get an anchor tattoo. She replied by telling me to look a little closer. As I put her wrist in my hand and pulled it up to see, she continued, "Do you see the scars underneath? I used to be a cutter, and I would cut my wrist. But once I stopped I wanted to get the anchor tattooed over my scars to remind me of hope." I put my arms around her and gave her the biggest hug. She had no idea how much her two-minute testimony touched me!

That's what I'm talking about! When you start to focus on the HOPE more than the HURT, God will bring healing to your heart. He will guide you step by step into the life you are waiting for. It doesn't happen overnight. Healing can be a long process, but if you allow Him to take you through that journey, you will never regret it.

Chapter 16

So that is my story. I am now the Director of Evangelism at my church and have the awesome privilege of leading people to Christ. I struggled for a long time with my past and wondered many times if I was even worthy enough to help further His kingdom. But God has reminded me over and over that I am exactly where He wants me to be. The prayer my mom prayed for me so many times—"Lord, whatever path Nanci takes, please let it end at the cross"—has been answered, and I know He continues to lead me and teach me His ways.

There are many days I wake up wondering why my life was spared, why I'm not a part of the videos they show at the Victim's Impact Panel, or why I'm blessed with the life I have. I have no real answer other than God is a God of second chances. He sees the good in us when all we see is the bad. He uses the weak to lead the strong and blesses us in the meantime. I will always have a hurt in my heart for Mr. Nelson. There isn't a day that goes by when I don't think about that night. But I have made a promise to Mr. Nelson and myself that I will do my best to carry the message, and I pray that many people will be blessed by the life he lived and the life he gave.

Mr. Nelson's sacrifice was like Christ's, only Christ sacrificed His life for each and every one of us. He overcame the same world that causes you and me to stumble. His love never ceases to amaze me, and I am humbled to be His servant. So I've made that promise to Him first and foremost that I will live for Him the rest of my days. Not as someone who's got it all together—I know I'm far from that. I simply live as a sinner trusting God and trusted by God to further His kingdom.

I wonder what my life would have been like if I had never gone down the road of addiction. There have been many times I was jealous of my friends who had the "normal" life. Kids who went to college right after high school, got married, and then had their children. Their lives always seemed so easy and almost perfect. "Why couldn't I be like them?" or "Why did I have to screw up?" I would ask myself.

It took me a long time to understand God doesn't want me to be like anyone else. He created me in His image and has a purpose for my life. I realize now, the places I went, the people I was around, and the hurt I experienced, taught me the importance of being a witness for Christ. God created me so I would be a light in the world. After walking through the valley of the shadow of death, I experienced firsthand the world without Christ. The lies, the deception, the selfishness, the pain, and the reliance on drugs to feel free and new—all of this a false sense of HOPE. Our world needs Christ—the only true hope there is!

One day I was driving to work and decided to memorize the 23rd Psalm. I wanted to be able to quote it when I was having a bad day or in need of encouragement. As I memorized the scripture it was as if God's voice was telling me, "Nanci, I am all you need, no matter what you go through; I will be here to guide you. I will guide you along the right paths, trust me. Even when you go through hard times, I will not only be there to comfort you, but I will prepare a feast for you. I will anoint your head and remind you that you are a child of God. I will make your cup overflow with blessings, and I will pursue you all the days of your life. And in the end, Nanci, you will dwell with me in my house forever." "Wow!" I thought. "He will do all of that for me even after I chose to live without Him for so long!" I don't have to live in fear or regret anymore. After all those years, I have just begun to understand what true forgiveness is. I am no longer a drug addict living in fear and dreading the next moment; I am exactly who I was born to be—a child of God, filled with love and *High on Hope*! "Therefore, if anyone is in Christ, he is a new creation; the old has gone, the new has come!" (II Corinthians 5:17).

As Months Turn Into Years

Your time on earth was all too short,

Your family full of tears.

How often you will come to mind

As months turn into years.

I've cried for you, with heavy heart,

Too many times to count.

I've thought about your family too

And how they live without.

Mr. Nelson, how I long,

To see you face to face

And tell you how you changed my life,

And taught me about GRACE.

Were you scared? Were you in pain?

The questions flood my mind.

Were you worried and thinking of

Your family close behind?

I'm sorry, I'm sorry, I can't say it enough,

Please know what's in my heart.

I'm forever grateful, for the life you gave,

For me, a brand new start.

I think of you, as a little boy,

A sweet and innocent child.

I think of you a fearless teen,

Curious, but mild.

I think of you as a loving dad,

Smiling from ear to ear,

I think of you as a sweet Granddad,

Whose family loved so dear.

I think of you with Jesus now,

What joy must fill your heart.

I think of you with no hurt and pain,

I think of your new start.

I think of what you've done for me,

and it blesses me each day.

Thank you for the life you gave,

That helped me find my way.

I know I don't deserve this life . . .

It should've been me, not you.

But I promise to live for both of us,

In everything I do.

By Nanci J. Johnson

57013477R00111

CPSIA information can be obtained at www.ICGtesting.com
Printed in the USA
LVOW051700290612

288113LV00002B/41/P